Original title:
The Plum's Pathway

Copyright © 2025 Creative Arts Management OÜ
All rights reserved.

Author: Matthew Whitaker
ISBN HARDBACK: 978-1-80586-256-7
ISBN PAPERBACK: 978-1-80586-728-9

Flavors of Found Footsteps

In the garden where jokes bloom,
Silly fruits dance in their room,
One wore a hat, another a shoe,
Laughing at the sky so blue.

A plum thought it could fly high,
Claiming the clouds as its pie,
It jumped and twirled, oh what a sight,
But landed softly, not quite right.

The pears threw a party, their tunes so loud,
With berry guests feeling quite proud,
They jived and jiggled, sparked such cheer,
While an apple decided to shed a tear.

But then a worm joined, quite suave and slick,
Said, "Don't be sad, just share your trick!"
They rolled and giggled, a wild parade,
In this fruity world, no fun would fade.

Legacy of Luscious Trails

In a garden where fruit often shimmies,
A squirrel decided to up his committies.
He danced with the berries, a bold little chap,
Until he collided with a big, cozy nap.

The grapes gave a giggle, such sweet little clowns,
While apples rolled over, avoiding their frowns.
A pathway of laughter, with fruits feeling grand,
Creating a legacy, all fun and unplanned.

Unsung Harvest Tales

In the orchard a rumor began to unfold,
Of bananas in jammies, quite wacky and bold.
They swung from the branches, quite the sight to behold,
Telling tales of mischief, ripe and untold.

Cherries on scooters, sped past the green grass,
Zipping and zooming, oh what a gas!
The harvest was silly, not just sweet and neat,
Creatures of laughter, a delicious retreat.

Fruitful Journeys

Peaches in helmets went on a small ride,
They rolled down the hill, giggling side by side.
Along came a watermelon, bouncing with flair,
Cracking up endlessly, joy filling the air.

Pineapples huddled, avoiding the bees,
While lemons played tricks, with humorous tease.
In a world of delight, where flavors unite,
Fruitful journeys beckon, under stars shining bright.

Sweetness in Twilight

As dusk settled down, with a wink from the sky,
The fruits gathered round, to share a good sigh.
The oranges joked softly about their bright hue,
While kiwi sang ballads, with rhythm so true.

Midnight snuck in, with a cheeky little grin,
Bananas in pajamas sang, let the fun begin!
Twilight was sweet, full of giggles and charms,
As laughter rang out from their magical arms.

Underneath the Bark

Underneath the bark so rough,
Critters play and call my bluff.
Chasing dreams of juicy bites,
In the sunlit, shady nights.

Squirrels plot with cheeky glee,
Running circles 'round a tree.
One said 'Let's take a chance!'
While the others just danced!

The Longing of Ripening Days

Days grow long with sunny rays,
Patience wins in quirky ways.
Counting spots that start to blend,
As I wait for sweet to send.

Birds chirp tales of fruity dreams,
Plotting schemes and sweet ice creams.
Each giggle fills the air with cheer,
Ripening fun is finally here!

Journey Through Aromatic Lanes

Aromatic lanes we stroll,
With smells that take a happy toll.
Bumbles buzz, with hearts so light,
Dancing under stars so bright.

Sweetness in each step we take,
Laughter ripples, hearts won't ache.
As we sip from nature's cup,
Bidding sour times to shut up!

In the Company of Blossoms

In the company of blooms we cheer,
Petal fights and pollen near.
Blossoms giggle, waving free,
Sprinkling joy for you and me.

Laughter echoes through the air,
While butterflies dance without a care.
Together we'll create a fuss,
As we sit on a nectar bus!

Harvested Dreams

In the garden, we trip and fall,
Chasing visions, we laugh through it all.
With baskets in hand, we dance in a spree,
Picking ripe dreams, as sweet as can be.

The sun laughs loudly, its rays like a song,
Turning our fumbles to laughter so strong.
In this merry chaos, we find our delight,
Harvesting dreams from morning till night.

Routes of Crimson Fruit

Down the path where the cherries blur,
We've steered our wagon with a little whir.
Our route's a circus, oh what a sight,
Bumping and bouncing, with sheer delight.

The crows cheer us on with a beak and a squawk,
As we wobble and giggle, a talkative flock.
Every splash of red brings a new little joke,
We tumble and tumble, like its some kind of folk.

Essence of Harvest

In a field where the fruit is wild and free,
We gather our stories, just you and me.
Each berry we pluck holds a laugh or two,
Essences bursting, so juicy and true.

As baskets overflow, so does our cheer,
We tease and we chuckle, not a hint of fear.
The essence of harvest, it's clear in the air,
It's not just the fruit, it's the joy that we share.

Juicy Road Ahead

The road's lined with treasures, a colorful spree,
With every step forward, what fun there will be!
A slip on the gravel, I laugh as I glide,
Juicy surprises just waiting inside.

The wind gives a giggle, the trees start to sway,
While squirrels join in, they want to play!
With each twist and turn, a fruit-filled delight,
On the juicy road ahead, everything is bright.

Nectar of the Earth

In the garden, fruits collide,
Buzzing bees, I cannot hide.
Fruits like plump pillows, so divine,
Each one screams, 'Come taste, it's time!'

A squirrel swings by, with a daring leap,
Grabbing a pear, making me weep.
He winks and scurries, oh what a show,
As I chase him, 'Hey! You stole my dough!'

Grapes giggle as they roll away,
'Catch us if you can,' they say.
Banjos strumming on a vine,
Nature's party, oh so fine!

With sticky fingers and happy grins,
A taste of laughter, where it begins.
Juices flow, the joy is real,
In this fruit festival, we all squeal!

Bruises and Brilliance

Bouncing berries, what a sight,
Some are bruised but feel just right.
A raspberry declares, 'I'm tough today!'
While a peach rolls off and slides away.

Bananas slip, and giggles cheer,
'Watch your step!' the fruits appear.
Oranges laughing, their zest on fire,
Making juice jokes, never to tire.

Grapes wear sunglasses, oh what style,
Fashion trends that make us smile.
'Bruises are beauty!' they chant and boast,
In this fruity play, I'll raise a toast!

So join this oddball gang of glee,
Where fruits collide, wild and free.
In colors bright, they strut and prance,
Living each day like a silly dance!

A Dance with Ripeness

Peaches twirl in the summer sun,
'Let's hit the dance floor, everyone!'
Bouncing apples join the beat,
With twists and turns, oh what a feat!

Berries shimmy, oh so small,
Doing their jig, they have a ball.
Crimson cheeks and fruity feet,
Turning this gathering into a treat!

Cantaloupes roll, grapevine swings,
While watermelon serenades and sings.
In this orchard, friends unite,
For a dance-off under the moonlight!

Laughter echoes, joy ignites,
As fruits unite on starry nights.
With every bounce and every sway,
We share in the fun, come what may!

Twilight on the Fruitful Trail

As the sun dips low, shadows stretch,
Fruits whisper secrets, ready to sketch.
Moonlit pathways, a joyful spree,
Where apples chuckle, as light as can be.

The night brings magic, laughter's glow,
Cherries tumble, putting on a show.
They giggle and bounce, 'Catch us if you dare!'
In this fruity frolic, without a care!

Berries tell tales of the day just gone,
Swapping stories until the dawn.
With starlit sprinkles and fruit-scented dreams,
Each moment's sweeter than it seems!

So dance with me on this whimsical quest,
In a world of flavors, we are blessed.
Twilight's magic brings a smile,
As fruits unite in joyous style!

Beneath the Blossom Canopy

Beneath the trees we laugh and play,
A plump surprise could blow away.
With each step, we dance and twirl,
    Hoping to find a juicy pearl.

The bees buzz by with a cheeky grin,
    As if they know the fun we're in.
We chase the blossoms, pink and white,
And taste the sweetness, sheer delight!

A nearby squirrel steals our loot,
Each nibble worth its weight in fruit.
We shout, "Hey, that's our snack to munch!"
But all he does is laugh and crunch.

So here we sit, the day so bright,
With laughter ringing, pure delight.
Under this canopy we dream,
Where nature's whimsy reigns supreme.

Ripening Dreams

In gardens bright with colors bold,
We spy the treasures, ripe and gold.
Each fruit just begs to be set free,
A bouncy ball of jubilee!

We dream of pies and sweet delights,
Yet all we find are silly bites.
A worm plays tag, can't catch us though,
Our giggles echo, up they go!

The sun beams down, we feel so fine,
As juices drip from tree to vine.
We laugh and share a silly dance,
With every fruit, we take a chance.

Then off it rolls, a daring feat,
One juicy ball just can't be beat!
We chase it down, oh, what a spree,
A cascade of laughter, wild and free!

Juicy Echoes

In twilight's glow, we hear the call,
Of juicy echoes, sweet and small.
With every step, we feel the cheer,
As fruits begin to disappear.

A berry bounces, oh what fun!
We race along, two girls, one bun.
As giggles ripple through the air,
We toss the fruit without a care.

Then came a splash, a sticky mess,
Surrounded by bright fruitiness!
With laughter loud, we slip and slide,
In juicy chaos, we confide.

Yet still we grin, and share the feast,
With every bite, our joy's increased.
These echoes linger, sweet and clear,
A fruity friendship, always near.

A Voyage of Juices

Set sail aboard a boat of fun,
Our oars are made of plump and spun.
We navigate through rivers sweet,
With squishy snacks for us to eat.

The waves of juice, they splash and spray,
As we embark on this grand play.
Each sip delivers giggles bright,
Our voyage turns from day to night.

A friendly fruit bat joins our crew,
He flips and flaps, what a view!
And as we sail on juicy tides,
We sing and laugh till laughter hides.

Yet storms may brew, when peaches fall,
We dodge and duck, then laugh through it all.
The sweetest trip, it can't be missed,
On this wild ride of fruity bliss!

Life's Simple Harvest

In a garden where laughter blooms,
The fruits are dancing, chasing rooms.
A squirrel steals a snack or two,
While bees wear hats, quite trendy too.

The sun's a jester, bright and bold,
Tickling the leaves as stories unfold.
While worms break out in merry song,
Each root's a dancer, hopping along.

Watch out for the crows that tease,
With their cawing jokes about the peas.
They've got a plan to snack and play,
In this harvest dance, they'll steal the day.

So grab your basket, join the fun,
In this nutty race to catch the sun.
Life's simple harvest, full of cheer,
With giggles growing throughout the year.

Sweetness in the Air

On a breeze that tickles the nose,
There's something sweet, as everyone knows.
Candy clouds drift in the blue,
Chasing the sun and tasting dew.

The trees are hums, like poppy tunes,
With fruit that dances beneath the moons.
And if you look, you might just see,
A giggling peach swing from a tree.

The ants hold a parade with pride,
As blueberry floats roll side by side.
They march in step, they sing, they cheer,
Creating sweetness in the atmosphere.

So grab a whistle, join the throng,
In this fruity festival, you can't go wrong.
For in the air, the joy is clear,
Sweetness lingers, spreading cheer.

The Delicate Balance of Light

In the morning mist, the sun does play,
With shadows that dance in a silly way.
A grape rolls down the sunlit street,
In a race with laughter, oh what a feat!

The light does jiggle, it winks and shines,
Making giggles spill from the vines.
While cherries flip in a game of tag,
As dreamy clouds try not to lag.

Each beam a dancer, swaying with flair,
In a ballet of light that fills the air.
The garden chuckles at the sight,
Of fruits that twirl and twinkle bright.

So lift your spirits, let them soar,
In this light-hearted romp, there's always more.
Where laughter mingles with rays so bright,
In the delicate balance of radiant light.

Labyrinth of Sweetness

Through twists and turns, the path unfolds,
To a maze of treats and stories told.
Where jelly beans line the secret ways,
And chocolate rivers sweetly blaze.

Silly rabbits hop in glee,
Navigating through a candy spree.
While licorice bridges sway and sway,
Leading to fun in every way.

The laughter echoes in every nook,
As gummy bears plot the next great book.
Each step is joy, with crumbs to share,
In this labyrinth, light as air.

So join the quest, don't miss your chance,
In this world of sweets, come take a dance.
With every twist, there's joy to find,
In a labyrinth of sweetness, joy's entwined.

Sweetened Footprints

A squirrel danced on the ground,
With the sweetest treasure found.
He slipped, then tumbled down the hill,
His cheeks blew up with jam-filled thrill.

In a tree, a bird did laugh,
At the picky pear's tough half.
But as he reached for that delight,
He fell right down, what a sight!

Beneath the branches, ants explored,
Carrying crumbs, their tiny hoard.
They slipped and slid through gooey mess,
While laughing loud, no time to press.

This frolic leads to sticky feet,
As laughter echoes, oh so sweet!
A chase for fruit, so big and round,
Our silly friends are joy unbound!

Blossoms and Bittersweet

In a garden full of blooms,
Bees buzzed as they met their dooms.
One took a sip, too deep he went,
And landed where the flowers bent.

A raccoon took a wild leap,
To reach the fruits all high and steep.
With a flip, he missed, alas!
He tumbled down like clumsy grass.

Oh, the taste was worth the fall,
With every bite, he had a ball.
But sticky paws and tangled blooms,
Led them straight to a patch of brooms.

Laughter spread through fragrant air,
As creatures shared without a care.
They feasted on both sweet and sour,
In the garden's silly hour!

The Path of Tender Fruit

A hedgehog rolled along the way,
In a jolly jam parade today.
He slipped on berries, bright and fresh,
And turned into a fruity mesh!

The turtles joined, with shells so round,
They waddled through the fruiting ground.
One peeked up to see the sun,
And fell right in, oh what a fun!

A rabbit dashed for peachy joy,
But tripped on squash—the sneaky ploy!
He ended up in pumpkin's embrace,
And sat quite still, a funny place.

As laughter echoed through the crop,
The critters danced, they just couldn't stop!
With bites of fruit, oh what a treat,
They found their way with giggles sweet!

Echoes of Harvest Time

In fields of gold, the roguish crew,
Searched for treats, in morning dew.
A duck quacked loud, found corn to munch,
Then slipped right through—what a funny crunch!

A goat with flair jumped high and wide,
But landed on a pumpkin's side.
He rolled and spun, then found his way,
To harvest's joy, a bright bouquet.

A mouse held tight to a grape vine,
Thinking he could make it all mine.
But with a tug, he tumbled down,
And wore the fruit like a funny crown!

Through laughter loud and autumn's cheer,
The creatures gathered, year by year.
To celebrate what brings delight,
With echoes of harvest, what a sight!

Ripened Journey

A fruit so round, it rolls away,
Chasing squirrels who think it's play.
Under trees, we laugh and trip,
As juicy gems start to slip.

We race the breeze, but it just grins,
It knows the secrets of our sins.
With every drop, a giggle rings,
As laughter flies on buzzing wings.

The sunbeams wink, the shadows tease,
A game of tag with buzzing bees.
We dodge the dirt, we leap, we laugh,
Who knew fruit could cause such gaff?

When someone slips on gooey skin,
We burst in laughter, that's the win!
As laughter echoes through the grove,
Our fruity journey's in full trove.

Orchard Whispers

In twilight's hush, the trees confide,
Tales of fruit that slipped and sighed.
With every wind, a chuckle's drawn,
As ripened dreams wake with the dawn.

Squirrels scamper, plotting schemes,
While hidden fruit beneath their dreams.
Who knew a peach could play so sly,
With hidden seeds and oh-so-fly?

The grass is tickled by tiny toes,
As laughter spills where sunshine glows.
With every step, a fruit parade,
In the orchard, joy is made.

We gather 'round, all friends and kin,
As juice and giggles mix within.
The world's a stage, the fruit our props,
In whispered tales, the laughter never stops.

Beneath Glistening Leaves

Beneath the shade, a bounty lies,
With purple crowns and sneaky lies.
The critters peek, we play our part,
As fruit goes rolling, the ultimate art.

We spot a bunch, plump and bold,
With tender hearts, our stories told.
Oh, victory sweet, we fill our bags,
But trip on roots like silly fags.

Giggles abound as slippers fly,
Fruit flies out—oh my, oh my!
With sticky fingers and laughter loud,
We stand around, feeling so proud.

The rustle of leaves brings tales anew,
As each fruit whisper weaves a clue.
In glee we prance, let's seize the day,
In the orchard of life, come what may!

Sweet Departure

Our journey's end, with bags so full,
We bid farewell to the orchard's pull.
With every step, a fruit escape,
We laugh and hop, our joy takes shape.

The last one's ripe, a daring bite,
But squirted juice gives quite a fright!
We shout and spin, the moments flee,
As sticky hands declare, "We're free!"

The path behind, stories we tell,
Of plundered fruits and gooey spells.
With every chuckle, we dance away,
A sweet goodbye to the fruity fray.

Next time we'll come, with bags in hand,
To taste the joy of this lush land.
For in the laughter, and juicy fun,
Our sweet departure's never done.

The Caress of Summer's Breath

In the garden, bees do buzz,
They dance and hum without a fuss.
Plums are ripening, juicy and round,
They taste like joy that knows no bound.

A squirrel leaps with flashy grace,
Stealing fruit without a trace.
The fruits of labor swing and sway,
Summer's sweetness, oh what a play!

Laughter echoes in the sun,
While children dash, their giggles run.
Stumbling upon a sticky mess,
Plum juice drips—oh what a dress!

With every bite, a grin appears,
A splash of flavor, joy, and cheers.
Mom's in the kitchen, apron on tight,
Baking a pie that feels just right.

Echoes of Sunshine and Shade

Under the tree where shadows blend,
The summer sun is a playful friend.
A picnic spread with treats galore,
Plum tart is a hit; they all want more!

Sipping juice, we feel delight,
While ants march in, a funny sight.
With every giggle, laughter's near,
As juice drips down, we shout, "Oh dear!"

The dogs chase kids in circles wide,
While laughter echoes, we push aside.
Splat! A plum falls, a funny blunder,
Rolling away—what a ripe thunder!

In the shade, we rest and sigh,
With stuffed bellies, we let time fly.
A plump mishap, with sun-kissed skin,
We promise to do it all again!

The Hidden Nectar

A treasure hunt in a luscious grove,
Where juicy gems hide, oh how they strove!
With hands outstretched, we search with glee,
Finding plums, oh what jubilee!

The squirrels giggle at our quest,
Plum thieves in training, they are the best.
"Look over there!" a shout unfolds,
As juicy treasures by the hundreds sold!

With nectar dribbling down our chin,
Every bite feels like a win.
The laughter bubbles, oh what a scene,
Caught in sweetness, sticky and clean!

As dusk falls, the sun dips low,
Our laughter fades, our cheeks aglow.
We scoff at seeds, like little bombs,
Planning a plum fight—oh the qualms!

Footprints in Bloom

Upon a trail where laughter flows,
With every step, the mischief grows.
Children skip through fields of gold,
While juicy dreams begin to unfold.

A basket swings with wild delight,
Picked fruits are our ultimate right!
But one slips out—a wild chase ensues,
As we run after, in sprightly shoes!

Beneath the trees, we twirl and play,
In search of plums, we'll find a way!
With sticky hands and silly grins,
We'll count our wins with every spin!

As evening wraps us in its bliss,
We gather 'round for one last kiss.
Under the stars, we drop our cares,
With plums in hand, life's sweetest affairs!

Through the Canopy's Veil

Under the leaves, a squirrel pranced,
Chasing shadows where it danced.
With acorns in tow, oh what a sight,
He stole my snack, it took a fight.

Laughter echoed through the trees,
As I dodged a branch with ease.
A bird dropped a berry, quite the mess,
I slipped and slid, oh what a stress!

In the chaos, I found my groove,
Twisting and spinning, needing to move.
The sun peeked through, bright and bold,
Making every moment a sight to behold.

With friends who laugh at every trip,
We chased each other, we couldn't skip.
Through nature's chaos, we'd forever roam,
In trees we found our funny home.

A Brush with Juiciness

A berry burst, oh what a treat,
I dabbed it on, my fashion feat.
With nature's colors, I did adorn,
But worried if bees would come to scorn.

One buzzing close, thought it'd sting,
But all it wanted was a taste of spring.
We shared a laugh, that little guy,
Did a little dance, as if to fly!

Friends gathered round, with mouths agape,
"Is that the latest style?" they gape.
"Juicy chic" I boldly claimed,
While wearing fruit, I felt quite famed.

Then the juice dripped down my chin,
Laughter erupted, oh what a win!
In nature's runway, we did sashay,
With fruity flair lighting up the day.

Lush Whispers on Pathways

On a sunny day, the greens did sway,
Inviting us all to come out and play.
We strayed from paths, chasing some wind,
And suddenly it felt like a grand trend.

With a hop and a skip, we wiggled around,
Unruly laughter, the joy was profound.
Then someone tripped, flying through the air,
Like a wobbly doll in need of repair!

Worms in the dirt started to giggle,
As my friend fell, it made me wiggle.
Brushes with nature, silly and loud,
Made us feel like nature's proud crowd.

Throughout the journey, our spirits soared,
Packed with memories that we adored.
The pathway's secrets, hilariously told,
In lush greenery, our laughter rolled.

Beneath the Canopy of Dreams

Beneath the trees, a dream I'd weave,
With pixies dancing, you wouldn't believe!
A little frog croaked, "I'm quite the star!"
But slipped on a leaf and fell from afar.

"Try again!" I called, grinning wide,
He took a bow, blushing with pride.
The branches above began to sway,
With giggles from critters joining the play.

Marshmallow clouds floated above,
And squirrels debated who could shove.
With nuts in hand, they formed a team,
Making mischief like it was a dream!

Through tangled tales, we listened near,
Each story shared brought toast with cheer.
Beneath the canopy, full of glee,
We penned our fables, wild and free!

The Language of Trees

In whispered tones they sway,
Telling secrets of the day.
Their branches bend, a jolly dance,
While leaves giggle at their chance.

Roots deep in the ground they tease,
Sharing gossip with the breeze.
Bark jokes that make the squirrels laugh,
A comedy of nature's craft.

Sunlight tickles every leaf,
Creating shade where we find relief.
A crinkle here, a rustle there,
Nature's humor fills the air.

So if you'd like to laugh out loud,
Join the trees, they form a crowd.
In their presence, joy is found,
With every rustle, laughter's sound.

In Search of Tasty Memories

All around, the fruit hangs low,
A treasure chest in sun's warm glow.
I barter bites for giggles shared,
With balmy breezes, none compared.

Each memory's a juicy bite,
In every taste, the world's delight.
I munch on laughter, sweetened dreams,
In every crunch, the sunshine beams.

The quest for flavors leads the way,
As laughter chimed in bright array.
From berry blush to citrus bright,
Each nibble brings out pure delight.

So come along and share a plate,
With memories sweet, let's celebrate!
In every taste, a tale unfolds,
A wanderer's feast, in joy retold.

Immersed in Citrine Shadows

Beneath the trees, I find my place,
In dappled light, with sun's embrace.
The shadows dance, a playful sight,
A waltz of citrus, pure delight.

Each step I take, the laughter swells,
In tangy scents, the joy compels.
With every twist, the whispers flow,
As laughter bubbles—'go with the flow!'

When shade invites a snooze or two,
The dreams are bright—like morning dew.
Awake from naps to citrus cheers,
In fragrant bliss, we banish fears.

So bring your friends and join the fun,
In citrus shadows, we all run.
With sunlight streaming, laughter's gleam,
Together we weave a joyful dream.

The Orchard's Heartbeat

The orchard hums a silly tune,
Where fruit and laughter bloom in June.
With every thump of falling pears,
A giggle bounces through the airs.

The trees are up to pranks, it's true,
Dropping treats for me and you.
A laughing sprite climbs up a trunk,
He ensures the ripe ones aren't just junk!

With every step, I find a rhyme,
In this fruity land, I savor time.
The winds carry jokes from branch to ground,
A comedy in nature's round.

So come and skip along the lane,
Where apples spin in joy, no pain.
In the heartbeat of our green retreat,
The orchard's laughter feels so sweet!

Glistening Shadows

In the orchard, shadows sway,
With giggles hiding in the hay.
Bouncing fruits, a grand parade,
Watch out for pies—oh what a trade!

Glistening bots in fuzzy suits,
Dance around with golden fruits.
Clumsy bees, they trip and tumble,
Land in pies with stinky trouble!

A squirrel's dance, all loose and free,
Carts off snacks, oh let it be!
With wiggles, jigs, and wobbly laughs,
While birds just watch, their gossip shafts.

Underneath the sunshine's grin,
Pie fights break out, let the fun begin!
A chorus of laughs in fruity dreams,
Life's a jest—we're berry beams!

Pathways of the Orchard

On winding trails, we skip and run,
Chasing shadows, oh what fun!
A lopsided fruit, not quite a peach,
Turns the day into a comedy screech!

Sneaky rabbits, plotting schemes,
In search of carrots or whipped cream.
Tripping over roots, they make a fuss,
Who's losing now? Well, it's a plus!

The trees are laughing, branches sway,
Counting leaves, on this goofy day.
Watch out for birds with crumbs in beak,
Join the race, it's the fun we seek!

So let's parade through grassy lanes,
With giggles echoing like playful trains.
In this whimsical orchard we play,
Leave worries behind, let's be splay!

The Taste of Hidden Trails

In tangled vines, the fruits do giggle,
Each crisp bite ends with a wiggle.
A hidden trail, for friends to roam,
Find a stash! Oh, seeds of foam!

With every step, a funny surprise,
Juicy drips, oh how they rise!
The critters plot, they've got a scheme,
To steal our snacks, what a dream!

Chasing butterflies under the sun,
Laughing till we cry, what a run!
Grapes turn into bouncy balls,
Watch out for steeples, oh how it calls!

Join in the fun, grab what you can,
Toast the fruits with an air guitar plan!
The trails lead us to laughter and cheer,
With every bite, it feels so dear!

Serene Drop of Sun

A drop of sun, on leaves it plays,
Chasing shadows in funny ways.
Frisky fruits wiggle with glee,
Underneath the buzzing bee!

A cherry slipped on morning dew,
Got giggled at, oh how it blew!
Ripe and round, it took a slide,
A bouncy trip, on the joyride!

The breeze it sings, a playful tune,
With little critters dancing, oh so soon.
Every rustle, a laugh, a cheer,
Joyful trails, it's all quite clear!

So glide through orchards, take a leap,
In the sun, the jests run deep.
Every giggle—a glorious fun,
In this harvest, we're never done!

Nectar's Whisper

In the orchard where fruit flies
Dance on air with little sighs,
A bee lands on a plump delight,
Sipping sweet till it takes flight.

The birds squawk loud, an echo play,
As squirrels race in a nutty fray.
Fruits giggle as they soak up sun,
Each drip of juice a tiny pun.

A laugh erupts from an apple's core,
It tells a tale of a fruit much more.
From cherry dreams to peachy screams,
They scheme together in juicy teams.

So join the fun in this garden's glee,
Where nectar whispers, let it be!
With every bite, a joke unfolds,
In laughter's orchard, life's pure gold.

Orchard of Whispers

In the grove where laughter grows,
Trees play peek-a-boo, goodness knows.
The apples roll, a merry race,
While laughter echoes, we find our place.

The pears gossip, they surely know,
About a strawberry's silly show.
Each branch a secret to be revealed,\nIn this fruity world,
none are concealed.

A lemon grins, quite the bright chap,
He tells the berries to take a nap.
But berries giggle, staying awake,
With all the silliness they can make!

So dance among the trees so free,
In this orchard of whimsy, join me!
For in every cheer, in every laugh,
Lives a fruity tale on a leafy path.

Serenity in Stone

By the rocks, where silence reigns,
A brave little snail hops on trains.
But these trains are quite the fuss,
As stones giggle, their secrets discussed.

The lizards bask, plotting a race,
While moss grows a beard on a stone face.
In stillness, there's noise, a quiet cheer,
As nature chuckles while we draw near.

Peeking behind with mischievous glee,
The flowers erupt in a wild spree,
Their petals dance as they start to tease,
In this nature's laugh, the world finds ease.

So stroll along this stony way,
Where whispers of humor lead the day.
For in each crack, each crevice found,
Lies a joke waiting to astound!

Path to Fragrant Horizons

On a path where scents collide,
A lavender tickles, tried to hide.
A spice jar tips, a salt shaker laughs,
In this fragrant world, joy crafts.

Basil and thyme throw a feast,
With cooking giggles, they're quite the beast.
A garlic bulb winks with a sly jest,
Unveiling aromas that smell the best.

The marjoram twirls, a ballet dancer,
While chili peppers add a little prancer.
Each whiff a cackle, each breath a cheer,
From this savory trail, spread the cheer!

So take this path, let's roam and play,
In the fragrant horizons, come what may.
For laughter's spices spice up our lives,
In every corner, humor thrives!

Nature's Ripple Effect

In the garden, bugs all dance,
Chasing shadows, what a chance,
Flowers giggle, petals sway,
Nature's laughter on display.

Squirrels plotting with grand schemes,
Stashing acorns in their dreams,
Birds on branches in a row,
Chirp and chatter, stealing the show.

Streams that bubble, fish that leap,
Jump right in, take a dip, don't peep,
The frog plays tunes on lilypad seats,
While bees belt out their buzzing beats.

Sunshine spills like marmalade,
Creating joy in the glade,
Nature's chaos, all's a game,
In this wild, delightful frame.

Flavors of Forgotten Trails

On the path where berries grow,
Wandering snails move very slow,
Mushrooms make a silly face,
Waving hats in nature's race.

Jellybeans in wild disguise,
Try one, and you'll realize,
Nature's snacks can surely tease,
Gummy worms among the leaves.

Whispers float from buzzing hives,
Honey drips where sweet stuff thrives,
Sunset casts a golden hue,
On all the treats the forest chews.

Laughter echoes in the breeze,
As we munch on all we please,
Forgotten trails, full of fun,
Time to feast, we've just begun!

Dancing in the Orchard

Orchards host a lively ball,
Apples waltz, and pears enthrall,
Cherries twirl in red confetti,
While grapes bounce in giggles, ready!

Branches sway, the leaves hum low,
All the fruits put on a show,
Peaches blush, they start to spin,
As the dance floor welcomes kin.

Blossoms pop like party hats,
Bouncing friends and chitchat bats,
The cider flows like bubbling streams,
In verdant fields of fruity dreams.

Round we go, a merry chase,
Nature's fun is full of grace,
With laughter in the orchard bright,
We dance away the day till night!

Gathering Summer's Bounty

In the fields, we gather cheer,
Hands full of fruit, smiles ear to ear,
Watermelons rolling by,
Jumping up to touch the sky.

Tomatoes blushing, ripe and round,
As we feast on treasures found,
Carrots peek from muddy beds,
While butterflies dance overhead.

Buckets brimming, colors clash,
Berries tumble with a splash,
Lemonade stands sprout like weeds,
Here's a toast to summer's needs!

Even the ants join in the fun,
Marching back with goods they've won,
Nature's bounty, wild and free,
A harvest dance for you and me!

Beneath the Fruit-Laden Bough

Beneath the boughs, I sit in glee,
Watching fruits drop, oh what a spree!
A plump one falls and rolls around,
I dodge it fast, it's a fruity sound.

Squirrels leap by, all full of cheer,
Stealing snacks and holding them dear.
One took a bite, a juicy hue,
Now he's stuck in a sticky stew!

Birds chirp jokes, a silly tune,
They laugh at me, say I'm a goon.
But I just smile, in this sweet mess,
Living life with pure fruitiness!

So here I stay, come laugh with me,
Under this tree, just wild and free.
Every fruit is a giggle worth,
As I soak up the sunny mirth!

Lingering in Ripening Colors

Colors dance on branches high,
Purple splashes, oh my, oh my!
I reach for one, it slips away,
This game of tag will make my day!

A yellow one winks, plays coy and tough,
It teases me, saying, "You've had enough!"
But I won't quit, no sirree,
To snag that snack is my decree!

Green apples scream, 'We're all unripe!'
While red ones giggle, 'You're not our type!'
I chuckle back, "Oh hush, you jest!
I'll wake you up, you'll be the best!"

So I linger here, in vibrant hue,
With fruity friends and things to chew.
Each color's laughter fills the air,
Nature's palette, a funny affair!

Tasting the Light's Embrace

Sunlight spills on fruit so bright,
I take a nibble, oh, what a bite!
Juices drip down, tangy and sweet,
I'm in a mess, with every treat!

A yellow slice winks at me,
"Join my picnic, under the tree!"
I tumble and giggle, feeling so spry,
As ants march in, oh my, oh my!

The sun grins down, a mischievous chance,
As I chase cherries, a wild dance!
With every munch, my laughter grows,
Swatting bugs and striking poses!

In this embrace of light and fun,
Fruit feasts sizzle; I have just begun!
So gather round, me and my snack,
Let's laugh together, there's no lack!

Reflecting in Nature's Mirror

In nature's glass, I peek and see,
A berry slick with laughter's spree!
It winks and nods, I burst out loud,
This mirror shows a fruity crowd!

Oh, what a sight, a silly bunch,
With sticky hands and a munchy crunch.
I pose just right, a fruity star,
"Look at us all! We're bizarre!"

Reflections ripple, my giggle's shared,
As fruits and I, we're all unprepared,
For this wild ride on nature's whim,
Serving up fun, we dance and swim!

So here we are, just me and my fruit,
In laughter's mirror, none is astute.
Nature whispers, "Join the jest,
Life's a fruity, funny fest!"

A Symphony of Ripeness

In orchards bright, a dance begins,
With fruits in hats, twirling like spins.
A jester's laugh in every bite,
Each burst of juice is sheer delight.

Bouncing round, the ripe ones cheer,
Merry melodies fill the air near.
They giggle and roll with no care,
Tiny drummers tapping everywhere.

Nature's jesters, plump and round,
In juicy antics, joy is found.
They play hide and seek in the sun,
Each fruity grin, a silly pun.

Oh, swing along these branches bare,
With fruity friends, we'll brave each dare.
In this fruity jest we smile bright,
Creating laughs from day to night.

Journey Through Lush Groves

In green cathedral, laughter swells,
With giggles rising like magic spells.
Each step an echo, squish and slide,
Oh, what a juicy, jolly ride!

Prancing through the leafy maze,
We stumble on our silly phase.
With every pluck, we strike a pose,
As juicy treasures spill and glow.

The squirrels wink, they know the score,
Unruly fun, they ask for more.
On this wild quest, we chase the sun,
Skipping, sliding, we're never done.

So grab a basket, fill it fast,
In this lush grove, we'll have a blast.
With every laugh, a splash of cheer,
Our fruity journey brings us near.

The Harvest of Heartfelt Moments

A mirthful harvest, who would guess?
These fruity giggles, a joyful mess.
With every wave of fluffy fluff,
A tale of laughter, rich and rough.

In baskets piled, our jolly cheer,
A bounty bright and feeling near.
Each fruit a pearl, a story spun,
In sunny laughter, we become one.

Tickling vines as we weave and roam,
These moments sweet, they feel like home.
In every bite, a memory blooms,
Laughter lingers in fruity rooms.

As twilight falls, the shadows play,
We toast to levity, come what may.
In this heartfelt harvest, love's our glue,
With joyful sighs, we bid adieu.

Secrets Beneath the Skin

In wrinkled skins, there lies a tale,
Of fruity secrets in the pale.
Smiling faces, hidden glee,
With every peel, we dance with glee.

What's inside? Oh, come and see!
A world of flavors, wild and free.
With squishy hugs and juicy sighs,
Each bite reveals a sweet surprise.

In laughter's grasp, we let it all flow,
Sticky fingers, where did time go?
These fruity jokes, they light our mood,
In every chuckle, joy's renewed.

So take a risk, just peel away,
Within those skins, our hearts will play.
The secrets shared, a fruity grin,
With every laugh, we let love in.

Branches of Reflection

Upon the tree, a plump delight,
Hanging low, just out of sight.
I stretch and reach, but miss it all,
Darn those branches, why so tall?

I ponder fruit, I ponder fate,
Is it ripe? Or must I wait?
Swaying gently in the breeze,
They laugh at me, those silly leaves!

The birds gossip, oh what a tease,
As I dance round the trunk like a breeze.
With every twist and turn I make,
I'm just a fool with no fruitcake!

In the end, despite my plight,
I grin and giggle with pure delight.
For life's a game of sweet surprise,
Branches mess with all our tries!

Paved in Fruitful Colors

A pathway bright with shades of cheer,
Where every step brings laughter near.
I trip on moss, I slide on peel,
Each stumble's worth the fruity feel!

Colors bursting all around,
Like confetti scattered on the ground.
I laugh so hard, I miss the signs,
Who knew fruits could cause such rhymes?

A squishy downpour, a juicy clash,
Everywhere it's fruit-flavored splash!
I skip and hop on this delight,
Paved by nature, oh what a sight!

Along this lane, the frolics grow,
With laughter lurking in the flow.
What's that? A berry? Oh, what fun!
My pathway leads to laughs, not done!

Treading the Vintage Soil

In earthy boots, I tromp and play,
Through ancient soil of yesterday.
Each step I take, a squeaky sound,
Muddy mischief all around!

With vintage roots, I take my stance,
The veggies giggle, join the dance.
I pass a gourd, he winks at me,
What fun it is, this jolly spree!

I dig a hole, in search of gold,
But find a worm, oh brave and bold.
He grins a grin, with dirt-caked charm,
His wriggly moves cause quite the alarm!

Yet in this earth, with tales so grand,
Every chuckle makes the day unplanned.
I shout hooray for soil's sweet toil,
In every laugh, I find my spoil!

Shadows Beneath the Bloom

Beneath the blooms, the shadows play,
I whistle tunes in a goofy way.
Caught in a dance, I trip and whirl,
Nature giggles, gives me a twirl!

The flowers sway with silent cheer,
As butterflies flicker near to hear.
Each lovely shade, a hidden joke,
In laughter's arms, I feel the poke!

I ponder petals, oh so bright,
How do they bloom without a fright?
I'm shy with pollen, a silly sneeze,
A cloud of bloom makes me feel at ease!

Yet shadows linger, teasing me,
With every move, they're wild and free.
I laugh along, beneath the sky,
In that funny space, I'm always spry!

Love in the Orchard

In an orchard bright and vast,
Two lovers picked fruit, having a blast.
They tripped over roots, oh what a sight!
Their laughter echoed as day turned to night.

With baskets overflowing, they shared a joke,
As a squirrel danced by, carrying a spoke.
They tossed him a berry, he didn't retreat,
But winked with mischief, considering a treat.

Back at the picnic, they made quite the mess,
Juice on their shirts, they could only confess.
Their hands sticky sweet, in love's silly world,
Where laughter is king and happiness swirled.

So if you wander where fruits dangle low,
Remember the orchard's love-fueled show.
For amidst the trees, where romance might bloom,
Life is a circus, not just a costume.

Sip of Autumn's Glory

In a corner café, sipping cider so hot,
I knocked over my snack—oh, the chaos I brought!
With a laugh and a grin, I danced on a chair,
While apples around me rolled everywhere.

The barista chuckled, pouring with flair,
Said, "Careful with that, it's not a fair chair!"
I held my mug high, like a champion champ,
Started a toast, like a campfire camp.

But the cup was too full, it tipped toward my lap,
"Just a sip!" I declared, but took quite the trap.
With a splash and a grin, I made quite a scene,
"Autumn's just spicy, so don't be so mean!"

And outside the window, leaves danced to cheer,
As my cider mishap drew laughter near.
For laughter's the spice, and fun's the best score,
In the season of colors and silliness galore.

Savoring Seasons

The seasons parade, each with its flair,
Winter's cold breath, stacked snow everywhere.
But come springtime, I trip on a bloom,
Literally face-first in a floral costume.

Summer brings picnics, joy on the grass,
I tried to impress, but I fell on my... class!
With sandwiches launching in glorious flight,
Who knew a good lunch could cause such delight?

And then fall arrives with crunchies galore,
I stomped on the leaves, and came back for more.
But beneath the crunch, found a lost shoe,
Maybe that's why everyone's chuckling too!

So here's to the seasons, fun's ever demand,
Each misstep and laugh, life's a playful hand.
In the orchard of life, joy's what I reap,
With a chuckle and jest, my heart takes a leap.

Enchanted Fruition

In an enchanted grove where giggles reside,
I plucked a ripe fruit just bursting with pride.
But it rolled down the hill, oh what a chase,
As I raced after it, what a funny face!

With squirrels onlookers, all chattering glee,
I tripped on a root and fell into a tree.
My head in the leaves, with berries in hair,
I laughed at the sight—was it style? Who cares!

Then a rabbit hopped by, with a wink and a hop,
"Hey buddy, that fruit isn't gonna stop!"
I jumped to my feet, feeling way too spry,
Chased after my snack with a determined cry.

So in this magical place where mishaps abound,
Every stumble and root means I'm already crowned.
For laughter's the magic, and joy's what's in bloom,
In the orchard of fun, there's always more room.

The Journey of the Round Fruit

A round little fruit rolled out one day,
With dreams of adventure, hip-hip-hooray!
It bumped and it bounced, causing quite a scene,
In a world full of laughter, so funny and green.

Through gardens of veggies, it twirled with glee,
Saying, "Catch me if you can!" to a bumblebee.
It dodged all the pickles, it laughed at the jam,
Just a cheerful little fruit with a wacky plan.

It leaped over puddles, did flips in the sun,
Chasing after the laughter, oh, what fun!
In fields of wild daisies, it spun in delight,
This round little fruit was the star of the night.

So if you see a fruit rolling with a grin,
Just know it's on a journey, let the fun begin!
With giggles and wiggles, it dances away,
A round little fruit, living life its own way.

Colors of Fall's Embrace

In the trees, the leaves started to chat,
"Look at me! I'm orange!" screamed a fat cat.
"I'm red and I'm sassy!" barked a brown leaf,
While the yellow ones giggled, oh, what a relief!

The wind played a tune that tickled their toes,
While piles of colors replaced summer's prose.
With rustles and tumbles, these shades took their flight,
Making fun with their friends from morning till night.

They tumbled together, an accidental race,
One leaf tripped a squirrel, oh, what a place!
The sky laughed aloud, as colors did twirl,
In hues of pure joy, giving trees a swirl.

So here in this season so lively and bright,
Each leaf had a story, each moment a sight.
When colors come dancing, you can hear nature sing,
In this fall embrace, life's a glorious fling!

Petal-Kissed Footsteps

Tiny petals poked out to dance in the breeze,
A parade of colors, made by the trees.
With each gentle step, they whispered a song,
Laughing together, where flowers belong.

A ladybug twirled; she took to the air,
"Watch me! Look here! I have nothing to wear!"
"You're perfect!" yelled daisies, all giggly and bright,
While sunflowers swayed in pure morning light.

A curious bee joined with a joyful buzz,
"Let's play a quick tag, just because, just because!"
They charged through the garden, giggles in bloom,
With each silly chase, they banished all gloom.

So frolic, dear petals, and dance through the day,
When laughter's your outfit, you do it your way.
On this path of pure joy, let's prance, let's sing,
Where petal-kissed footsteps can't help but bring.

The Dance of Fruit and Foliage

In a dance-off of flavors, the fruits took the floor,
"I'm the juiciest one! No, I'm better!" they swore.
Bananas were bustin', and berries were bold,
While apples just twirled, claiming crowns made of gold.

The leaves joined in too, with a rustle and sway,
"We're the best part of the fruit buffet!"
Grapes chuckled softly, sharing the fun,
"Let's twist in the sunshine, till day's finally done!"

With smoothies and salads, the party took flight,
What an outrageous scene, oh what a delight!
Pineapples spun 'round, with a tropical flair,
Said, "Join in my dance! No one else can compare!"

As the sun set low on this joyful charade,
The fruits and the leaves made the whole garden parade.
In this wild fruit fiesta, let laughter resound,
For in every ripple, pure joy will be found.

Horizon of Sweet Delights

A fruit on a tree wearing a hat,
Swaying gently, oh fancy that!
Ripe and round, with a giggle or two,
Tickled by breezes, in a dance so new.

With neighbors so juicy, plotting a heist,
Chasing the sunlight, they think they're nice.
But little do they know, as the worm in disguise,
Can't resist a sweet bite, oh what a surprise!

Lemon's sour face, it's pulling a prank,
While cherries are rolling, they're starting a bank.
One little plum just dances around,
Singing a jingle, a fruity sound.

On the horizon, where silliness swirls,
Berries in capes doing twirls and whirls.
Glancing at clouds, they think they can fly,
As the sun laughs, saying, "Give it a try!"

Fruitful Pathways

A raspberry in shades, soaking up rays,
While a peach tells stories of golden days.
They skip down the lane, making merry and jest,
Only to find apples planning a fest.

A strawberry winks with a cheeky grin,
His buddies all giggle, the fun's about to begin.
A watermelon slides down with a splash,
Creating a scene that's a total smash.

"Be careful!" shouts lemon, but it's too late,
The fruit bowl erupts in a wild, sweet fate.
Bouncing and laughing, they tumble and roll,
What a sight, a fruity parade in control!

Across the orchard, the laughter resounds,
Joyful together, no worries or bounds.
With flavors and colors, their friendship is bold,
These playful delights, their stories unfold.

The Symphony of Harvest

In the orchard, a band of fruit starts to play,
Melodies of sweetness to brighten the day.
Bananas on drums, with rhythm so tight,
While the kiwi sings high, a comical sight.

The pear tries to dance but trips on a vine,
Falling down softly, saying, "I'm fine!"
Peaches are laughing as they roll on the ground,
Creating a symphony of giggles around.

As berries join in, they pick up the beat,
Each one adds flavor, a tasty retreat.
Harmony found in the laughter and sound,
With every fruit jamming, a joy most profound.

At dusk, they all gather, a fine fruit parade,
Sharing their secrets, the jokes never fade.
Together they thrive in this orchards' delight,
With a song in their hearts that lasts through the night.

Sun-Kissed Adventures

Under the sun, grapes wear shades of gold,
Planning a caper, a story to be told.
With bold little peaches donning fresh flair,
They set out on adventure, with laughter to share.

Through rows of bright green, they go hand in hand,
Searching for mischief in this fruity land.
"Catch that banana!" someone giggles with glee,
As they zip past the radish, quick as can be.

Through puddles of juice, they splash and they play,
Not caring at all what the oranges say.
Glorious sunshine, a pathway of fun,
Everyone joins in, the laughter's begun!

At the end of their journey, they bask in the glow,
The fruity brigade, putting on a show.
With memories sweet, they settle down tight,
In the orchard's embrace, till the next sunny night.

Moonlit Reflections on Skin

Under moonlight's gentle sway,
A fruit once decided to play.
It rolled right down the hill,
And caused everyone a thrill.

With laughter echoing so bright,
It dodged the cat, a sudden fright.
A slip, a slide, it took a chance,
In the night's absurd dance.

Jokes were made about its fate,
Should it bear a royalate?
But alas, it just plopped down,
Creating giggles all around.

So gather round, both young and old,
For stories funny to be told.
A fruit's life, so wild and bold,
Under moon's gaze, pure gold.

Beyond the Garden Gate

Past the gate where weeds conspire,
Lives a radish with great desire.
It dreams of being veggie royalty,
But finds itself in kitchen loyalty.

A carrot laughs, "Don't you see?
You won't be king, not yet, not me!"
With dressing too thick for a throne,
This radish feels so all alone.

When summer's light shines overhead,
They play tag, no time for dread.
The garden blooms with laughter sweet,
As veggies dance on wobbly feet.

So next time you munch on a snack,
Remember the radish and its knack!
A royal twist, a playful jest,
In gardens where laughter's the best.

A Fruit's Silent Story

In the bowl sat fruits of flair,
One with charm beyond compare.
No royal title, just a grin,
A fruit that dreamed it could win.

It whispered tales to its friends,
Of gardens where the laughter never ends.
"Let's have a party," it would say,
But nobody knew how to play!

So off it rolled, a daring ride,
To find some fun, not just abide.
It hit the floor with such a thud,
Causing giggles, pure fruit flood!

Now each fruit tells the tale of cheer,
Of friendship forged when laughs are near.
In silence, they share the gooey spree,
An epic quest for hilarity!

Whispered Tastes of Yesterday

In whispers soft from days gone by,
Fruits reminisce, a dreamy sigh.
"This pudding's great, but do you recall?
When we held the grand fruit ball?"

They danced on spoons and swayed on plates,
Creating flavors that thrill and elate.
But one slipped off, a comedic fall,
"Oops, my dear, not so regal after all!"

Tarts and pies share secrets sweet,
While crumbles rejoice and move their feet.
With every bite, nostalgia swirls,
In kitchens, laughter twirls and twirls.

So savor each nibble, each crumb of zest,
For memories made, we are truly blessed.
In every flavor, there's a smile's trace,
Whispered tastes always find their place.

Serendipity in Silhouette

On a sunny day, what a sight,
A fruit fell down, oh what a fright!
It rolled and bounced, then took a trip,
Right into the pie—sweet, what a slip!

The squirrels debated, debated all day,
Should they indulge or let it play?
With wrinkled noses, they cast their votes,
In the end, they danced with pies, not odes!

A juggler juggled juice so bold,
While acrobatic ants laughed at the gold.
With silly hats and fruity cheer,
They guffawed at plans turned into smear!

As twilight painted skies with glee,
They relished the chaos, oh can't you see?
With plums of joy in their tiny paws,
The day was won with silly flaws!

The Journey of Soft Skin

There was a fruit with a grand design,
Who claimed he was utterly divine.
With a wiggly wiggle, he strutted bold,
"Look at my sheen, I'm worth my weight in gold!"

His friends, they chuckled, "Goodness, oh me!
You're smooth as butter, but don't act so free!"
Then slipped on a peel in a wild ballet,
And rolled into the jam, what a silly display!

They hosted a party under the trees,
With giggles and grins carried by the breeze.
The soft-skinned hero, now covered in glee,
Spun tales of his slip—a top shelf marquee!

In the end, they toasted with zest and zest,
To the fruity fool who just couldn't rest.
As they savored delights, the sun took a bow,
And the night drifted in with a giggling vow!

Arc of the Orchard

In an orchard where mischief liked to play,
The branches swayed, come what may.
A plump little lad with a penchant for mischief,
Placed his foot in a basket; his style was quite stiff!

The wind whooshed by with a chuckle so light,
As fruits began tumbling, such a ridiculous sight!
They rolled down the hill, a circus in bloom,
Creating a conga line, oh what a doom!

A rabbit in glasses gave directions for fun,
"Keep rolling, keep rolling, till the day is done!"
With a flip and a flop, they danced their own jig,
While the raccoons clapped, all dressed in a fig!

The dusk brought a calm, with lamps that did twinkle,
As the fruits finally settled, and stopped with a sprinkle.
They swapped tales of their wild, fruity spree,
And laughed at their antics, oh so carefree!

Wandering with Boughs of Abundance

A fellow with dreams of sweetness and cheer,
Set out one day, with nothing to fear.
He packed up his knapsack filled full of prunes,
And hummed a soft tune to the light of the moons.

With boughs that bent low, he met with delight,
Where laughter echoed in the broad daylight.
Each fruit had a story, a flip, and a giggle,
As they shared their secrets, they danced with a wiggle!

A toad on a branch wore a hat made of leaves,
While revelers mulled over sweet there's-eves.
"Let's jump in the basket!" shouted a pear,
As they toppled and tumbled without any care!

In the end, they pondered their comical quest,
With nuggets of joy—now that's the best!
As stars sparkled bright and the evening was bold,
They toasted to laughter and tales to be told!

The Unraveled Journey of Sweets

Once a little fruit, round and small,
Decided to roll, had a great ball.
With a giggle and tumble, it lost its way,
Chasing bees buzzing, led astray.

A picnic was planned, oh what a mess,
Ketchup and mustard, all in distress.
"Who needs a plate?" chuckled the glee,
When fruit salad danced with hotdog bratwurst, whee!

Bouncing and bobbing, it laughed so loud,
While ketchup dodged, and mustard was proud.
A splash in the bowl, a plop on the floor,
Fruits mixed with condiments—who could ask for more?

At last, it was saved, in laughter and fun,
A bizarre buffet where all could run.
With friends all around, no longer alone,
The sweetest adventure, a flavor well known.

Mellow Murmurs

In the garden where giggles grow,
A shy little fruit put on a show.
"Pick me, please!" it said with flair,
But it rolled away, losing all care.

A squirrel came by, wearing a hat,
Said, "Oh dear fruit, let's have a chat!"
With laughter they danced in the bright sun,
Murmurs of fun, oh what a run!

Birds chirped tales of silly delight,
While ants in a line danced left and right.
The fruit learned to groove in the warm breeze,
And welcomed the friends as they bent the trees.

With a wink and a grin, it found its place,
Among giggling greens, a humorous chase.
Together they laughed, in whimsical cheer,
Creating a melody for all to hear.

Nature's Tapestry of Flavor

A riot of colors on nature's stage,
Fruits wore their flavors, penned their page.
With a zing and a zing, they had a ball,
Joining together for a fruity free-for-all.

"Who's the juiciest?" a peach called out,
While lemons and limes laughed in a rout.
They juggled their seeds, with a giggling fling,
Nature's own circus, oh what a swing!

Down by the creek where the wild things roam,
Mangoes slid down, made the water their home.
They splashed and they flopped, in a fruity spree,
"What's better than water?" they shouted with glee!

When day turned to dusk, under skies so bright,
They twinkled like stars, a marvelous sight.
A tapestry woven with laughter and cheer,
Flavors intertwined, oh what a year!

Savoring the Journey

Rolling along with a curious crew,
Strawberries grinned, while the blueberries flew.
Through valleys and hills, a jig and a jig,
Bananas chimed in with their funny big wig.

"Onward!" they cheered, teetering with grace,
Tomatoes blushed bright, in a fruity embrace.
Kicking up dirt, and hopping in sync,
They mixed up a potion that made everyone wink.

A pit stop they took to munch on some cake,
But the frosting giggled, "Don't make a mistake!"
With sprinkles that danced and cherry on top,
Everyone laughed as they made a great flop.

When the journey was done, they gathered in glee,
A feast of bizarre fruits, so funny to see.
Savoring moments, the joy of the roam,
With flavors and fun, they found their sweet home.

www.ingramcontent.com/pod-product-compliance
Lightning Source LLC
Chambersburg PA
CBHW060123230426
43661CB00003B/305